Moonlight is Better than Sunlight

Harley Rose

It's okay because,
We're all perfectly imperfect
We all have flaws that make us unique

DORRANCE
PUBLISHING CO
EST. 1920
PITTSBURGH, PENNSYLVANIA 15238

Dorrance Publishing Co
585 Alpha Drive
Pittsburgh, PA 15238
Visit our website at www.dorrancebookstore.com

ISBN: 979-8-8868-3157-3
eISBN: 979-8-8868-3735-3

For

My mother who loves the flower that holds the meaning of love,
The Rose

The Lunar Moon is for You and I

The moonlit night bares no everlasting fate,

Only watching people grow night after night.

Brightly singing a sleepy tune as two people fall fast in love.

Summer was just around the corner,

And the green tree leaves pop out beautifully,

Like a starry constellation that's mixed within the midnight blue blanket.

Voices begin to fade since it's becoming late...

Ever so lightly, you walk the night alone like a whisper..

The night wind blows ever so gently,

As a memory I cannot touch upon replays itself gently..

I lay in bed looking out my window,

The moon seems so lonely like myself,

But how come is she still so bright?

I'm scared but I think I'll be alright,

For I must remain strong.

I hold my necklace for comfort as I try to remember you but only slightly.

The sun will soon be rising,

The once blue sky will become orange and red.

Why must the magical glow of night leave us all behind?

The night is a mystery of beauty; one not everyone tries to explore.

I bet you'll think about it now when you're staring back at your own shadow!

Is the world big enough for everyone truthfully?

We take both the alluring sun and graceful moon for granted,

But why must I wish to hear the moon's melody over the suns?

I am one that holds a nightly aura.

Everything is quiet and different as time seems to stand still..

Fireworks now burst open along with a scent of grief...

One that makes me cry out of bittersweet joy

The moon sings and cries along with me as she watches me grow up..
And the midnight skyline is nothing I wished for but —
I quietly made a wish on one beautiful shooting star on the night of a full moon.
As my heart left my chest I breathed very slowly but hopefully at the sky.

The Monologue of a Teddy Bear

It's okay, I understand why
You left me alone in that grassy field..
That day was very much
History or so to speak...
It was a Monday
When I became too heavy.
Stuffed too much, my love.
Was I too much to bear for you?

A child whom I give comfort to.
When you fell and scraped your knee,
We'd dress up as Western Cowboys
But I'd prefer dressing up as dragons and princesses!
The many nights where you feared the dark
Or when I'd come for causal tea
I'd be in your imagination,
Yet physically there for all to see.

Making your days go by better with each installment.
Hum to me, I'll listen.
Read to me, I'll share.
Dance with me, for I cannot move on my own.
At night when you fear
Cry into me, for I am there.
I love you human, did you not love me too?
Was I a silent burden?

I am a bear, made of fluff,
One that depended too much on your childish love..
Forgive me for speaking out of turn.
But was I? When you grew up,

When you left me there,
Alone... Was I finally a burden to you?
This thought does not leave me blue with the Monday Blues
For everyday is now blurred by a blue abandonment.

4 - Harley Rose

On That One Night

Let us scream at the sun
For it would never be ours.
On the night I once wished to die,
There was no shallowness to beware of

I held no greed or pain
Why was there no rain
To wash away the colorless plain
To bring a colorful soul back to root.

I felt so lost and alone
In a frock so out of touch..
Colorblind I was —
Yet I saw everything so very clearly.

All ears and eyes of others were boxed
Blood came from their mouths
They no longer owned their tongues
I didn't wish to be in such a humane world.

I cried a river in the chest of my dolly
Fear of happiness consumed me
Emptiness and darkness crawled
I walked and walked until I couldn't find my home

On the night I didn't die,
My heart broke
Yet I still always travel with hope I dare to have —
Despite the sorrow I own

Lolita

Lolita, come to me.
Show me my true self in heaven
Where no vain or materialized matters
Even in modern or medieval bigotry.
How is it that not many know of your name?

I am nothing. And yet I have everything!
I have value, a voice, and a look to appeal to many
But am I truly what I appear to be?
So one with fairness then again ever so miserable?

Messages upon your arrival came!
Forgive me Miss Lolita,
But please forget my gracefulness.
I'm not what I wish to be
I'm not where I want to be.

Lolita, let me go.
You're in your own room of displeasure!
Don't give into the most with that disturbing advantage.
Today I strike, for my lonesomeness has reached its point.

Now I shall shut down.
No more wittiness, compassion or passion.
I shall grow slowly becoming one with my own company
Who needs friends? Not I.
I have no want for anything, for anyone, except for you, Lolita.

6 - *Harley Rose*

A Liquid Solitude

The many lands would be all mine
How shallow and selfish of me?
The infamous world of silver waters
A wonderful luxury left reserved
I'd own it all in an act of kindness
Where a simple dream became my solidarity..

Solitude, would be my pleasureful friend..
In life, in ink and by the silver diamonds of inspection.
In the meantime nothing but wildlife can bring peace,
No boundaries to roar on about agony.
Pearls forced me to wait patiently
Where I sat alone by the lake in solitude..

September 3rd, 2021

My mothers sickened candle flickers
To grow a light unknown.
Feathers of a bird makes me laugh,
Peeking a smile I never knew I could own.
I'd love to burn to flames in this fire
Which I call it, my inspirational grief
A microphone to make one's voice heard,
A microscope to see the cells,
Calculate the burns
Fake it all, no I must own it all,
For I am nothing
But a growing flame of fame

8 - Harley Rose

Unmanageable

I should have killed myself when I had the chance,
I now watch her choke
On the cigarette she smokes.
My death is near yet I do not fear
It would be a freedom filled luxury.
My manic episode led you to panic
Yet don't be scared
My words most favorable
True and all,
Actions natural yet then again
A trigger is one thing
A daydream of satisfaction came to me
Where I imagined her head
Spinning backwards
Eyes shot, blood loss
I love her I do,
Yet how can one feel something towards someone
When both of us own our own toxic motivations
And do not care nor desire one another.
Fake it I do with all,
It's too bad she gave me life
One I so badly dishonor

Waiting to Soar

Identity is something truly unknowing,
It's a mystery all on its own for you and I..
To wake up to a new day,
But without any educational success despite how hard I try.
I'm impatiently waiting for —
A passion so grand that I wish to have.
I can't seem to get along with those who are my age,
Which leaves me without much hope,
As I shatter my mirror so I don't have to look at myself.
I'm sad whenever I'm told that I'm intelligent!
And I walk waiting for something to hit me —
Hit me like lightning! What a feeling it would be..
I am a character that I still need to figure out..
But I know who I am but I'm left waiting,
And there is no right or wrong for us black sheep and black birds.
I dream of jumping so that I'll fall then fly and soar!
A black sheep who became a scapegoat,
The black bird that people run away from
As we symbolize true individuality and haste freedom!
I'll clip my wings but I will not bite my tongue!
I will fight and I will find freedom
But not for myself but for everyone else..
All I need is the open opportunity to jump.

Our Own Wonderland

Within a room of serenity.
Smoke draws one into illustrations.
One's vision can be mistaken for hallucinations.
After the pipe fell and shattered,
While there is only one man with a deer head,
You see four of him dancing.
Promise me you won't cry in spring,
I beg you because you'll make the flowers cry.
And as butterflies pass by,
How pitiful that you're now lost in a state of insanity,
While we're all sane.
"Don't you dare try to be ordinary" they once told me but —
Heaven won't find us because we're not extraordinary enough.

We have no heroines.
Our trousers and blouses were changed to dresses and petticoats.
We're still entering a room covered in ink,
Red roses roam the grounds.
What was full of serenity like tranquility has lost its touch.
Running to catch the pipe's replacement,
Within my drunken dazed state,
I tell you "I love you" something I find hard to say.
The clock moves backwards like time normally wouldn't.
Colored smoke calmly begins to fill the air.
Kiss me gently but don't when I say "No"..
Holding me close means you're perfect....
As dry lightning hits near,
I lost my key to my door of dreams.
Alone I am and lost I was,
I still look at you and your beautiful eyes.

Lying isn't for the path we once conquered.

Who is sure that we are even real?

People always used to point and laugh at me.

Why can't I be more *'ladylike'*?

At times I think I am not in my prime..

Who could even love me?

A young lady of the court I would be

If I wasn't true to myself. But who even am I?

And as I walk day after day down the same old street,

The rain washes away my doubts that heavily waver

Alone in rage I become very pale and dangerously mute.

The Deer Head Man shot an arrow just nearly missing me,

And I don't know what is wrong with me in your eyes.

One day, I promise that I'll be ten times more extraordinary,

When I start to grow apart from you..

Being a black sheep can lead to real future happiness

As we branch into our own worlds,

I'll always love you.

Love is Rare

I watched as they betrayed me..
My gears break — like death came quick.
The garden is dead and wilted.
Our expensive expectations we put out there,
Only to get hurt by all but one.
Vergence is worthless much like friendship,
But love is rare -
So we protect ourselves and our love
For when such emotions and time
Unexpectedly happens
This time, like all the others I was wrong
To accommodate for a rare and powerful giving.

Time Was Made To Rot

Let's begin quickly and move fast,
'Cause the hourglass has one last hour of sand to tell
The tale of the one I wanted to harp on about.

No clock is truly honest,
Time is a gauntly man who wears many worn silks
The very one that makes my guilt show slight compassion with a smile.

Two weeks I wished I had to finish my quest!
The world is slowly pausing and muting
I'm getting rather antsy because —

I couldn't do anything but wait!
So let's Riot! It's the last hour of earth!
And I'll wear what I wish as I kiss my reflection 'goodbye'.

Be who I want as I experiment before you.
Nothing but a dream of mine that became true,
No true wildness could be tamed tonight.

And it feels so good to me but bad to you.
Where is the miracle of a wish when you need one?
Maybe for once, my biased opinion of sunlight and moonlight will change.

As the last seconds I spend here,
The hourglass has gone completely empty...
All of the riches couldn't change that..

And with a snap of my fingers everything crumbles
Now with nothing left to charge for,
Within mere seconds Earth became a wasteland of time.

Misappropriation

One misappropriation, one wild night
Became that of a mockery the mockingbird sang.

As we sailed the seven seas,
Explored worlds that are not our own.
Underground where the dead still roam
An everlasting party they hold.

As I choke on my own vomit,
My head spins like a spinning wheel the elder spinster overworks.

On this cold night, my last breath
Is nothing more than a mockery to you
As you all continue to dance and party
No lies or whispers can be heard in the chill of one's terror filled wails

It's Okay For Me to Be Locked Away

I sometimes wished to have a companion
Then again, why waste time on something,
Filled with weakness and one day sorrow?
I'm good yet I buzz around
As my negative personality kept me apart
My confinement that many call a prison
I love it, it can turn my screws..
To force myself to talk — takes much caffeine
To be myself takes nothing at all.
While I express such love and appreciation
At the end of the day,
In the maze we call a path
It's pathetic.. I walk away from the light
To unattach the hook I held on to.
Music will be my greatest foe
Books shall be my greatest friends
Words shall be my greatest lovers
And knowledge will keep me sane
As I dream of closing off the world.
With my cellphone battery on 10%
I have nothing to lose

Promises Break

The air is now broken for our time has come,
Yes, it came rather short.
And the breeze caused my path to be blocked off.
Today came with haste and tomorrow left in peace.
You wanted to meet, to make a reservation with me but —
Making a promise will break me.
Now a portrait hangs aloof in your dining room
Sensually thinking nothing much.
Sparkle like the night,
Forget the rotation for a moment.
Let's join hands if we can all be simply kind,
I was too much of a fantasy
To promise you I'd stay seated for long
Let's practice a dare only to be safe
What pride it would bring..
But a broken chain may prevent us from coming true

Mortal Beauty

As my mortal soul begins to leave my body,
Lady Liberty who is coy can no longer hear my voice,
Which calls for thee
Unless we were to be a dolce luxury
Where satisfaction won't be found —

Beware of what they believe you to be
The truth lies behind that door,
Forget about the scale and magazine for a moment.
A rope is being knotted as we speak.
There is nothing to act upon

I want you to paint me like the famous portraits in museums
Is this so much to ask for?
Give me a glow up,
Don't you dare photoshop!
Didn't you hear? I hate it when you compliment me.

My soul now roams the earth unbound,
Without the chains of control
The beauty within
Cannot showcase itself due to the 'invisible laws'
I was never able to be the docile lamb.

Listen, are you listening to me?
I want to inspire the world in a positive way,
I want to show the world my rareness,
My flaws which are part of my natural beauty inside and out
What makes one unique ; Let's break down walls...

The truth of what beauty is

18 - Harley Rose

It's nothing more than a lie.
Everyone and everything is beautiful,
But we're often numbered and told
"You can be beautiful because —"

My own mental sanity began to crumble
Just as my soul left my body behind,
My dearest cries for thee,
And due to society's standards,
A rope hangs around my neck for if I can't be beautiful, why should I live on?

The Time That Travels

Immortality, what a beautiful word
For thee who must desire,
Longing for adventure and ambition.
Many sadly go young,
Many wish to stay forever.
As some grow with time,
Her tears were like diamonds,
Mine were like a sea of sirens,
His were hidden by his hair.
Those who are beautifully immortal,
They're resilient only for themselves.
Within a 'non realistic' society,
These Immortal Souls are Pragmatic.
Unlike you and I at times of doubt.
Let's just breath and rid all of our unworldly chains,
And walk into the pond of true purity,
Where we'll bind ourselves to be silky.
For our own inner glow,
And if destiny is not disappointed tonight,
Maybe we too can gain Immortality.

All Our Lies are to be Sworn

I waited for Satan's carriage

Where the last stroke of midnight could be heard.

Not a sober soul could be seen from afar,

Not even beyond the creek where children once played

Nothing but the echoes of their summertime laughs remain.

When Satan's carriage arrived,

The door swung open most hostilely and his hand grabbed me

Pulling me into a Victorian-style delusion.

He lit a match once I was seated,

It smelt fruity and bitter within his carriage

Due to the pipe he smokes which makes him appear most human.

We rode down 5th avenue,

Passing by all the abandoned stores as two in the morning drew near.

And some people still roamed the streets,

To all, I and Satan's carriage seem to be invisible

Especially since he and I have business to discuss.

Even with his old fashion way of human life

Satan sees me as an equal.

Not as some dainty woman who's waiting on men.

As his carriage reached the end of the earth,

Satan kicked me out — there on the ground I now lay.

He refuses my interest and my advances towards his work sadly.

Satan loves me enough to keep me on Earth,

Lord Death his dearest friend, barely knocks on my door anymore —

As it seems that the Heavens and Hells always fight over whose bad or good.

Only where I wait for Satan's carriage each night,

I also wait for him to gain affection for me.

Checkmate, No Thanks

Come inside and look at my wall of desires please.
A board with red string,
It's like a crime scene
As the cameras flash
We're all just skipping rope on top of a chessboard.
My life is nothing but a grey fog
Despite my young age and happy look
I'm not saying that I may want to die..
But I am in agony of my own demons,
I'm nothing but a pawn to society's chessboard.
The King rules all — Yet sadly he doesn't show us his face!
Which means nothing but everything to me, his loyal subject.

We're all pawns at our own game of pace.
Wit won't get us anyway, not today.
Fire roars like a Leo in spring but I'm not brave at all.
Art opens the mind as I gamble away my own brain..
Gated inside, locked away but still my appearance is as grand.
Mentally screaming for help
Just as the subway train runs over my chest!
And everyone walks past me,
Achieving a dream or settlement
While I am left floating.
Sure I am publishing and studying,
But I'm not here, I'm nothing but close to a "checkmate" for the King..

The Queen gives me an order yet is scary crazy.
"Protect the King!" She roars as the Knights run and the Bishops dance.
But I can't just stay as a simple pawn in this game of life..
It's now twilight right before dawn
And we're now playing double dutch

Leaving us to be nobody's that's unknown as history echoes make us deaf.
Society will just have to do without me
'Cause I rather stay eccentric, I want to be seen as odd...
Much like the shadow inside of me is..
Love isn't for those who desire,
When it is I who must walk the road alone!
You won't achieve in buying me, I ain't worth a penny!
Sweetie, the rope has become dangled as all the pawns but I were captured..

Someone please give me a heads up..
I'm about to die alone
Which is better than living a life with people is it not?
I don't want to be a boring person anymore,
I'm annoyed then again I am chasing a light..
And I must admit, chess is a very boring game
I want to play cards without betting away my fortune
Although my solitude has been broken with eighteen..
Society has rules that are unfair that are also unspoken..
Social media is almost too much to bear
I'll break every single rule just as I paint my face with eyeliner
And I won't achieve a checkmate..

The Circus Performer

Here I am all alone staring at my reflection in the world's mirror,
Since I refused to paint my face like a clown.
I'm no ringleader 'cause there is no such thing as self control.
Stuck in the back hallways of many covered posters
My tent is always draped in the finest velvet.

Beyond the whereabouts of our stained souls that wait
The world is nothing but tied by a single red string of faith,
One with so many cuts and bruises.
Yet I don't want to believe that I'm an ugly one, one without a single dream.
People aren't weak nor vulnerable, we're all just caged performers!

Here I am trying not to shed a single salty tear,
Even with my strength I'm still as weak as an ant.
I wear nothing but sweat and blood as my master's motherly whip calls for me.
And three ladies dance around me with their fragrance of purity in silk
A new morning must arrive someday or I will have to run towards the sun.

Everything is feeling like a lost cause as I start to walk upon the tightrope...
Being this broken shouldn't be seen as a joke for entertainment,
Yet the circus audience would have me thinking otherwise.
I refused to press the repeat button to fade this horribleness away,
I wish I would drown in my bed sheets masked within my room's darkness.

Hearing the crowd's loud cheers. With nowhere else to turn..
Faking all innocence towards him
The Ringleader has a look of curiosity and cruelty in his eyes.
I feel as if I fall before him, I would lose everyone and everything.
Soon I heard dawn approaching, calling my real name where I lost myself..

I Beg You

As tears drip down my face,

Staining my cheeks..

I gently stroke your hair,

As you take your last breaths.

I cannot bear to say "goodbye"...

Please, I know you're meant to be with me,

As if we were too good to be true.

Winter will soon come,

And snow shall cover the ground.

I'll miss out on my happiness without you.

The kiss I gave doesn't help revive you.

You died right here in my arms.

I beg you to forgive me..

If you didn't follow me,

Everything wouldn't have ended like this.

Is it okay that I will pain this day forevermore?

March 20th / My Vegan Leather Jacket

Wanna know what bothers me most in life?
When things go missing..
Misplaced and lost.
It drives the human mind into distress.

Naturally messy, I am disorganized and will leave things around.
I remember better when the object I desire
Isn't where you'd think it should be,
But this item I lost — is of most value to me

My leather jacket, vegan leather.
I hang it on the end of my bed
Even when it fell, it always came back
Now in its time of need it cannot be found.

I went crazy looking through the mess I call a room.
All I own for space is the door, the closet, a dresser and my bed.
In my mess, about six-by-fifteen I say,
No leather jacket to be found.

It will show up when it wants to be found.
I know I haven't misplaced it,
If I buy another, the jacket would then show up.
I'll wear my denim for now and worry about my leather tomorrow

Astronomical

'Who am I?' There isn't a correct answer to give.
'Why was I born?' It is for you to figure out on your own.
I, for some reason, don't listen.
I won't obey you 'cause your words disappear from my ears.
I know for a fact, I'll never be what you want me to be.

Why couldn't we be on Mercury?
Close to the star we call the Sun.
Or maybe I have a twin like Earth,
Venus was once full of love inside and out.
Mars is colorful but hides in the shadows of its wars.

No one will ever understand who I try to be...
Polaris always points me to home.
The Vulpecula is quite sly, wouldn't you agree?
Ophiuchus bordering my birth sign, Scorpius
And this comet is poorly calling my name..

Jupiter has a storm that brews over and over again..
Saturn has many rings of pleasure to allure many eyes to love.
Many years ago, Uranus must've been bumped into,
I know how that feels..
Neptune's moon Triton may be its second in command..

A fellow man I saw from afar
Left me without much confidence in such a diamond rain.
Time became so infinite — non expensive yet nonetheless
I want to live in security despite being exposed.
My imaginations shall one day pass by one's Nebula wishing for beauty.

Chaotic Thoughts

The world is nothing but chaos

With a path that burns while on fire..

Bandages upon Bandages you wear,

As a child, your innocents played a role.

An ax is thrown at its target,

Shattering the clock made of glass..

Walking within the chaotic planes, I'm prepared to fight

Not knowing what shall come next,

Which scares me so..

I'm a tiger who is invisible which is used as an advantage.

Watching the sunset off a mountain cliff,

I soon turn and run back into the Jungle.

Nothing but chaos surrounds me,

Running passed trees, vines, fields of grass,

Wildlife noises are so loud I can't think straight.

Soon I'm lost in a maze..

My passion is becoming more and more real,

But I cannot love her, for I am a warrior

Within chaos

On January 2nd, The dandelion said...

The dandelion said to the pigeon,
It's okay to be unsure,
Make a wish for comfort,
I'll follow you through.
Just as the pigeon blew to make a wish.

Months later, the pigeon said to the lizard,
It's okay to be emotional,
It doesn't make you weaker,
It makes you stronger —
Just as the lizard wanted to cry.

Weeks later, the lizard asked the monkey,
"Are you happy?"
The monkey said "Not really."
The lizard asked, "Then why pretend?"
Just as the monkey was left appalled.

The monkey asked the shooting star,
"Why is life so lifeless?"
Only for it to sparkle.
Despite no answer,
The monkey felt a glimmer of hope

Supper Madness

I sit at the supper table — I tell myself to not engage.
'Because a conversation goes sour quickly.
All four were wrong and each mind was disheveled.
Screams were made, shouts were told.
Stupidity gathered and hatred of all four grew.
Yet despite this I still craved affection that was real.
Yet arguments become dyer
Food wasted and I no longer wish to speak
Grudges I do not hold
But tiredness consumes me like a damn trade.
Can't do anything nice,
Can't do anything bad..
All I can do is curse and say
"You people aren't worthy of my time"
Only to be told "Shut up"
While one makes a laughing sound - did she wish to tango with me?
Ugh, the sickness I felt and the glee of growth I had.
The aftermath I know will be much worse
I left the table — I engaged, which was my worst decision.

The Flaws of Creativity

A true artist can't control their mind,
Their emotions and thoughts are too loud.
Leading many into intense creativity,
One the dull world will never understand.

Artists can take inspiration from others,
Yet I found myself,
Falling too far into the darkness of someone else.
What a pitiful sight I bet it once was.

I had to allow myself to be destroyed,
So that I shall find a place of belonging,
Even though I haven't found it yet.
I still throw paint onto the canvas.

At night, my intrusive thoughts stain the oblivious floor.
My hands are covered in charcoal.
Paint brushes were scattered all over my room.
I cradle myself as I whimper wondering who I am.

A room with no hope,
Just a bit of class that peered from the window.
Oil paint staining my cheeks,
I softly ask 'when are you going to leave me alone?'

Voices crack nearly as a whisper- like sound.
I can't take it anymore,
I am trying to build myself up,
Only for her voice to tell me to "fight it, so it will go away".

But I shall have this forever.
As something red drips from my arm,
Just let me go and allow me to fall..
I am now allowing my mind to scream once more..

Tradition

The world moves slowly yet ghastly.
Traditions are made to be kept.
Traditions are made to be altered.
Insurance will not pay for the damage,
For her soul that was burdened by tradition.

She lays in her coffin where many come to say 'goodbye'.
Some cry, some gossip, some brought flowers but no god was to be found.
Now her ghost lingers not knowing what to do.
The world couldn't see her flare,
Her indifference was beautiful and yet too rare for many.

She would always keep you on your toes
Traditional people couldn't understand,
Tradition couldn't hold her down
They knew Tradition wasn't for her
So why force it down her throat?

At her funeral they blamed her,
Then again she was both right and wrong.
Her spirit sees her body laying still,
She walks away from the coffin,
No longer wishing to hear her family's wails.

Her spirit lingers on the earth she so dislikes,
Only to watch everything still move
She observes the reactions of –
The many people she haunts and the flowers that grow.
Breaking more traditions while even in her afterlife.

Nobody or Somebody

If I were to become somebody,
Would I still be the wallflower I am?
I won't lie, I am a bit neurotic.
All hope has disappeared for I am too tired to believe
And people still pass me, push me away unknowingly.

I'm better off as a nobody,
For my passion brings no wanted desires.
I still wouldn't be worth the effort
All I can say is "good riddance"
As I crawl myself into a hole I call my safe haven.

The Scorpion

As night came to be
Every flower in my room wilts to black
For I can no longer feel happiness
The warmth of his humor
The coolness of her music
And they were beautiful all on their own,
The four of us together.

I cry alone in awkward rage
Unhappiness consumes me
Like a poison from a scorpion sting.
Overthinking, over analysis, but relaxed.
I must stay hard on myself,
For I will no longer come to be friendly,
Like a rag doll I have a sewn mouth.

As the sun begins to rise,
I realized that I haven't slept for days.
I cry but it's all on the inside,
For no emotions must show.
I am not allowed to be myself,
So I play your way,
And that's not good enough..

Say it isn't true,
The garden is cold and icy much like the human heart.
Overthinking and misjudging yet scorpions know better..
I must keep my wall around me.
It'll be safer that way.
I let my guard down and I am now hurt.
So I'll forever walk like the ghost you wanted

The Masquerade

The Orchestra plays a symphony,
Which was bitter and sour like a lemon
Despite the song meaning to be sweet.
Which means that the melody is becoming more impatient.
As one's voice echos the halls

Beyond the Grand Staircase,
The opera singer waits for another,
Who would ever believe that she wasn't very lyrical?
The empty auditorium; saved for the orchestral musicians.
No words came from their mouths just as the show's about to begin!

Eyes cast on the blinding lights.
Not even looking at those dressed in the most expressive ball gowns..
They didn't even pay attention to someone's screams of pain
For it was hidden by the belts of each instrument in tune.
Such a tragic romance wouldn't you agree?

Tears came from his eyes, how can we save him?
An aria that was meant to echo beautiful power
Just happened to become very dramatic..
The night that was once peaceful
Now includes a harmony that has turned depressing.

The many books that lay upon the classic libraries shelves
Next to the room of regal portraits
Show me your true colors please
I want this bitter symphony to be over.
Fashion is changing in the audience just as the ballet begins..

The Red Swan who wails realized that,

The Orchestra was a beautiful façade
With a play of words and a play of emotional joy
Heartlessness did not rule this day but —
It was nothing but a beautiful Masquerade

The Insanity on Hell's Lane

Hell's lane makes you insane,
For you can no longer remember your name..
While all you hear are screams,
The many sounds come from those tortured souls,
Who are left to rot within the asylums walls

I ask for nothing from your god or mine,
Sitting on the floor holding myself in the dark,
All shaken up and nervous we are,
Our neighbors give us nothing but bloody screams,
That echo the isolated asylums walls

All they do is laugh and mock,
People are hurting more so than I,
I am said to be insane since I am nervous,
Wouldn't you be too if you were just assaulted?
This asylum is where children come to lose their souls.

April 16th / The Fool is I

I hate my fellow man-kind,

For all the pain, sorrow, the happiness they express

Even as I wish to experience many things,

Alone, hating the very thing that shows empathy.

I wish I wasn't born human,

I'm hating all mankind, not just a subject group.

Broken in a fast lane

Walking upon the highway during rush hour.

Why was I cursed with distrust and dislike past the "introvert status",

But to give compassion towards younger people,

I'll never admit that I am human,

I'm nothing worth much, I'm nobody and I like that.

Maybe I'm a fool to you…

A moment to shine, I shared to fit in,

Yet I never feel like I belong with anyone

That's because I'm a nuisance in a world overrun by the very thing I dislike.

I am a Writer

When I write I tend to lose control,
Then my own horrors and fears arise again.
While I just barely think, my hand scribbles words..
My passion grows by just looking at the same plain wall.

And so, they laughed
And they cried
As I sang happily off key,
Words randomly connect,
Growing richer with each stroke of my pen
Misunderstandings are better than nothing.

My dear sir, while you're such a division
A delusion of grace is what I can be.
Unreal we're such real things
For my blue eyes to sew lace upon.

My eyelids are becoming heavy at 5 in the morning
My flame is put to rest until I awake again.
Last thing I saw clearly was white,
When the sun blinded me,
Where they laughed
At what little confidence that I had left.

When I write I announce a repeating feeling,
Like the rhythm of the subway
And my room is so dim it's too dark to see.
Dawn is coming, locked in a pictured fear.

The Artist Behind the Mask

The Artist Behind the Mask,

It's me, don't you see?

As I sit in my shadowy corner,

Wearing my dark clothes and flannels

There is a very colorful and artistic nature inside of me.

Maybe I'm wearing all black and white,

But I see myself wearing a beautiful rainbow,

Full of creativity and hope,

You may try to knock me down,

And make me feel weak or afraid,

At times I do want to give up

I will become stronger.

As I see myself in a beautiful rainbow,

I know the world is tough and not always fair.

But if we are able to grasp knowledge,

And try to see the world from someone else's shoes,

Maybe one day, everyone will see themselves as their own Artist,

But unlike me they won't hide behind a Theater Mask.

Everyone with their paint brushes,

Will paint a beautiful rainbow

Lighting the way towards a new dawn

Life's Ignorance

Once on a stormy night
I caught you looking at the moon's dazed reflection,
Within that glass of water...
As one's childhood fades away.
People grow to lie with their fantasies
It's life versus death.
Thunder and lightning scares me so I hide.
And there is nothing to feel empathy for..
I ask myself often "who truly is human?"
Since I distrust them all.
As children run and laugh,
With their unknowing innocents playing a role.
As our vision becomes blurry,
The dark burden begins to creep in...
So I will write you this sorrowful hymn,
And keep my heart closed off,
Since you opened yours,
You were stabbed deeply and painfully.
And then I was covered in your blood.
But I won't cry, because my eyeliner took me all morning.....
I know I am an ugly creature.

The Many Seas of Words

Beyond the shore
Where the mermaids swim
Calling me to play with them
Freeing me from all my heavy burdens.
One day, you and I will dance in the park,
We already sit and mail letters to one another..
But for now, I'll stay with the mermaids
Who won't sing because if they do
I'll lose my freedom and my boat.
The sea never dies, it keeps flowing,
The sea keeps changing while staying the same.
Where birds fly and lizards creep
Bunnies hop and ducks quack..
There is nothing more lovely than a book.
The toxic air I once consumed my whole life is now pure.
So honey, let's forget the seven years of bad luck,
Just come and swim in the many seas of words with me.

Colorful Ambivalent

Let's not waste time to talk
As the world is very bleak.
Full of nothing but Negative Identities,
People walk unknowingly like zombies,
Looking back and not saying anything..
Each one programmed to either —
Get into their car, get on a bus or wait for the subway cart.
Just when all the local shops and delis open on the new morning street .

You can see the exception that runs through your veins
But ignore it we all do.
You wear brightly mixed-match clothing that reflects you,
But it's hidden under your neutral coat.

I have ran into a dead end of the world!
It is dark in front of the eyes that are torn onto me.
The zombie apocalypse has already started,
We're both in it but are trying to break from it -
If there is a wall in my way,
It shall be broken one day.
It was wrong for it to be built,
But it was made during the dawn of time..

How does one live with the past and future being so similar ?
How does one learn to compromise?
Can you teach me how to give the puppet way a try?
Maybe I am a catastrophe person.

I must find the exit that'll allow me to leave this society party..
As I dance between each person walking,
Crossing the streets, exiting the trains, buses and their cars!

44 - Harley Rose

Where do you wish to run away to?

I just thought I would dash quickly.

It's not like you'd notice if I left.

If you don't wish to come and be colorful,

You can stay here walking in the same circles that you've been doing since birth.

Philosophical Stargazers

Will you wait for me when this metamorphosis is over ?
I'm a lonely butterfly and all I can say,
I am a bit behind but not an idiot.

My sixth sense kicks in at the wee hours of the morning,
Strumming to a guitar you once were..
I'm sorry that I lag with feelings and can come off as robotic.
It's precious, our relationship.

Like the Little Dipper and Big Dipper,
You and I are like Andromeda and her mother Cassiopeia,
Way up in the sky, millions of miles away, detached from worry.

Loyalty works both ways,
And I must admit that there is nothing to fear.
You're precious to me even if I act dangerous.
I'm sorry I'm not what you wanted.

I can't sleep, but I can dream.
I can't feel or be happy, but I can be kind and patient.
If you're okay then I'm okay.

Artistry

Art is an escape.
It allows your mind to stop,
Become calm as you reflect.
And if you just pick up a pen or a pencil
And you don't need to think...
You're true soul will show,
While lost in the chaos of the storm
Whether you're hurt, happy, enraged, numb, scared or sad.
You're escaping everything...
Red Eyes are Glowing with Passion
Green Eyes Glowing with Envy
Art is helping you create a world where you feel safe,
And if you don't understand then you must not be colorful enough..

Domestication

Do I want to go on for all eternity?
A mess I am, don't domesticate me please.
Beware of what they call loyalty,
The river always changes sides when in battle,
No loyalty is to be given by it.

You had a dream, one of a life!
Sadly now you're transparent,
Sitting wearing a man's suit,
I am a woman but who really cares,
Calling all the shots but more invisible than ever before.

Society would have me forced into a corset
One not allowing me to breathe!
And your eyes will become dead and lifeless
Washing you away with the crowd
While I stand here detaching myself from blissfully thinking.

I stood in the center of the court of socialization.

The eyes of all parties were glued on me.

Not including my opinion or side in democracy is nothing.

I wait for my bail to be set.

Refusing to speak, refusing a lawyer, refusing everything.

A lack of humanity,

I felt the shade,

I held the sun and I grieved the many pennies I wasted on making wishes.

You might as well give up your soul

To hell is where I am sentenced to go

And that judgment is fact.

No respect is to be given when you're at fault.

Especially when you're "respected" by being straightforward

Judgment comes when people are elder than the younger,

Deeper the conversation

Makes the staircase more spiral.

In a courtroom filled with social creatures

I'll run away yet kept my feet glued to the ground

Become an actress and act as a character I most dislike

.

Falling into the tears of shadows,
I opened myself to you,
Can you see yourself?
My knuckles bleed as
I write these words to you,
Within a liar or a name,
Spring came, winter longed for me.
No one can be tamed,
Yet you can count on vulnerable honesty,
So if you playfully say I lied.
Don't shoot the messenger
The very one who sits upon the crescent moon
Especially if you ever met me in person,
I'm nothing but a fairytale.
I speak to all the same, I treat all the same.
So reader, my friend,
Follow me into the shadows.
I'll show you a world of fantasy, pain, and sorrow,
And I cannot help, as I'm haunted by words
That I must paint..

There Wasn't a Sound Except for my Conscience

There wasn't a sound
Except for my conscience
That told me otherwise

Despite its meaning to keep me in line,
My conscience wishes for me to rebel.
Intrigued by the tiger's eye.
Impulsive but steady.

The sound the trainer made,
Her voice is that of a snail.
While her dialogue was spoken quickly,
Her words made me move slowly.

My conscience was there when I acted good,
My conscience was there when I was bad
Leaving chills throughout your spine,
I earnestly wish to fall into your arms.

Dreams become a prize in a crash
But there wasn't a sound
Except for my conscience.

Letting Go

Don't leave me all alone,
It's snowing so heavily.
Within a world I created for my own,
To see you there,
I even start to cry,
Something I love is leaving so slowly.

I've driven my own growth away,
Soon winter will become spring.
The snow disappears as birds sing,
Happiness and joy,
What a beautiful picture,
You would laugh since I always sing off key.

Gently you console me,
Spring flowers soon meet the summer sun.
Laying there upon the grass,
We laugh about nothing,
Talking as birds fly high,
I wonder if you're truly real.

Living upon the other side,
Alternatively autumn flies into play.
Days go by with leaves dying,
I remember when we lived together lovingly,
Now we don't sadly,
Since I traveled to the other side of the Mirror.

Metaphorical Symbols

The man I saw on the subway,
He fell down the stairs,
Now, he shall die tomorrow.

He was holding a red rose which turned black.
As a black crow flies high within the sky,
My left boot has a dagger.

I cannot be drunken happy,
For life shall forever be a deadly lie..
Symbols abolish that death comes sooner than we think

The Death Verdict

Where the moonlight shines brightest..
I shall presume the Crucifix Position..
For that —
There shall be no tomorrow for you nor I.

Covered in darkness,
I don't wear black because it goes with everything..
It blends in with my personality,
And my fighting style.

Sometimes being invisible isn't as bad as it seems..
As I appear and disappear,
I am the Eyes and Ears.
Not loyal to anyone, but I have connections to all.

Our Lullaby

A song one sings like an Angel
It's that of a lullaby.
It's like a siren's soft cure.
Prepare to close your eyes,
This tune will help you dream

Before you can say 'Goodbye'.
Doves are love birds,
But you my darling are a deer.
I wanted to die ; You wanted to live
How queer that our lives became reverse

Once I wanted to stay in your arms
But I knew I couldn't fly to you.
The future I now can own
I fear that I'm stealing from you.
Before I leave you too within the sunlight

I can only hope that these words I added to your song
Will lead to one last soft kiss..
Light colored petals cover the woods as if they're snow,
Now, this lullaby is coming to an end
I hope that these words made you become everlasting

The True Irony of life,

Is nothing more than a bloody knife...

No one ever wants to talk

About something that stalks..

Pretending to live around it you wanted,

But it still ended up with you being haunted..

Just like in a story,

Everyone seems to know that will happen,

Only to be a misguided third party

For you don't know..

The shade of the shadows,

I can no longer see outside my windows.

We're being haunted,

Why am I being hunted?

Life is full of chapters of a story,

Not knowing what comes next..

Leaving a dramatic flair,

Led by a shadow sitting in his chair,

Watching.. waiting.

For he is longing to taunt us.

For he is longing to want us.

The Sorrow of Life

Black Bird in the sky,
The Raven flies.
The Raven is small and cute.
The Crow squawks in the daylight.
Flying high, seen but not heard.
As moonlight comes,
Midnight sadness pours over.
The Raven Cries,
For it's alone at the darkest hour,
Just as it was alone during the day

Doris and Light

Storming a lie to only tell the truth,
In a courtroom that is cracking and lacking in all but happiness.
Yet I'm not happy, I'm just well.
Surprise, the lighting strapped me —
Jumping out of my boots, pitter patter bittersweet.

How generous men could be,
But today no one can shine as brightly as I.
A mothers hand I wish to hold,
Yet I am the mother of words in light —
I am going to go walk across a broken bridge.

Dazzle to the sound of trumpets with me
Where hero's fly and ruin my plans, stay in the dark.
Unstable emotions of a late teenager I process,
Teen years are leading me —
To a bountiful day without a match to light my way.

The Last Text

Time stands still..

The rain stopped in place..

The cars no longer move..

Loyalty is something not everyone has for everyone.

Within your face I see your pain

Anger within your smile..

Your eyes speak to me saying you're one tortured soul,

Never will I regain what I once lost.

"A man must make painful choices"

But as a woman too, she must make painful choices..

I stand by you, holding on to you..

You're frozen along with time..

My watch starts to click,

And time soon begins again.

Alone I stand

My hand holding your face

A tear falls from my eye

I slowly backed up..

I turn on my heel so that now my back faces you.

Time starts again, and..

I run away, as you stand there confused as the cars pass by.

I gulp deeply as I run.

Weeks pass and I have never seen you again

My text that said "I'm on my way" was never sent...

December 13th / Winter's Divide

May the stars shine bright while you burn to ash,
That the winter forest will bring a dream.
Lit by many candles as icey lanes drive for acceptance.
Parties and celebrations with a feast beyond compare.

Joy for once won't be in vain..
My misery washed away with the sight of many snowflakes.

Eight candles for me shine bright,
A genocide of trees happens every year,
Blood is on all of our hands.
Then again what a jolly day to be with family and friends.

A bond of pride and truth — not even our parents can separate us.
Let's just build snow people and play in the snow..

Submissive

Our souls cut and raped,
The crimson blood leaks,
Hands covered with my own.
I'm nothing but a slave to my emotions .
Your will is so sexy but toxic.
Tonight, I'm so sorry for being weak
I need to end this relationship right now..
Am I a sinner? Or a saint?
I'm a Devil's Child trapped in a cage.
You and I laugh then wail.
We bathe in each other's blood,
And you're draining my life.
I'm in your hands ; I became Crimson Red
What a stoic expression you have,
Am I in pain? If so it feels good but not..

In Search of Something

My tower of insecurities is standing tall,
With hundreds of knives hanging over my head,
Wandering this temple,
Lost within its walls..
From behind a shadow
I hear your voice,
Followed by a sinful laugh.
I cannot find you..
As my feathers fall to the ground,
Weaker my body becomes,
As the Phoenix who once soared through the sky
Forgets that I was left behind,
Each turn I take,
A hall of mirrors I face.
The double life is one to play.
Walking old broken glass,
Despite everything I stand strong,
I am in search of something,
In search of you..

Changing Dragons

Autumn, a time of change came
As my passion and longing grows,
Even though I am only seventeen,
One step closer to womanhood,
One step further away from innocent years.

Blossoming I wish I was,
Yet I am mocked by my siblings.
Winter soon will become spring,
What once was cold and dark,
Shall warm up to be bright and life-like.

Wanting to grow closer,
But we must keep our distance..
I'm afraid to become a slave to my own emotions.
My emotions are dangerous,
Like Mr Dragon if he were angry or pissed.

Out of control
Living on the wild side but still playing it safe.
Now Summer is here..
With the long days,
The Sun is showering nothing but heat..

My feelings for longing are still there,
As if a change in me what's to be made
Sometimes fear holds me back,
But it also allows me to run.
I'm afraid of my older sister who only knows anger.

Blossoms come, bloom and grow,

Is all I can do... yet in her and everyone's eye I am "pathetic"
Why hold onto the past and try to renew everything?
"You're Beautiful" said Mr Dragon.. my mind went wired.
"I'm changing inside and out" I responded with a courtesy.

A Person's Misfortunes

Misfortunes keep may not be your own,
While one's sanity breaks,
Sadistic laughter uproars.

Hearts may be free to choose,
Birds see all as their feathers cover the ground.
I won't pretend that I'm perfectly okay,
When I'm not and I don't know what I am exactly.

Throwing things as one's mind is lost,
Within the Nightmares that creep, his laughter still lingers.
Your comments are unnecessary, truthfully they aren't needed.

Lilies dance within the wind with cherry blossom petals
Touching the pond ever so lightly.
Bravery and courage is keen,
Even when one is scared to face the world.

One's questioning when unwanted is bothersome.
I don't wish to talk about it because it's tiresome.
Since you don't know half of it.

And even if you did,
Forever it shall remain the same..
Just like everyone who lives on,
It's still my own misfortune.

A Poet is Supposed to Love, but I Do Not

Many speak that the poets know love

While I write of such emotion

I cannot think of love

Be suspenseful, wear a big smile

In flocks a plenty that bring light and shade to the world,

Personalities are then showcased day by day.

As I stand having people believe me to be a extrovert

I am not one of them.

I can love, but I'd rather be alone.

Love can blind someone,

And a young woman I knew once told me

"I don't allow my love to blind myself – nor should you"

So why do I need to be such a thing?

Why should I need love?

My heart couldn't take that pain.

Appreciation of glass that is stained

In the colors of passion and grace

That will bring us a new day.

I know the idea of love – but I do not care to show it to all.

I sit with my big heart open to all,

Yet closed off to all as I distrust everyone in society

To care and understand my instability

Venomous

Snakes full of Venom,
Slithering around me...
Demons in my mind laughing...
Nightmares glaring, toying with us
Scaring us despite us being the poisonous writer,
One oasis for desires,
Telling me to be honest with myself
"I feel alive" it wishes for me to say
As the snakes full of Poison wrap themselves around me..
Holding me, hissing within my ears,
"Playing" like my old wind-up doll..
Ink covering my hands,
My dress is covered with paint stains.
Soon as the sun rises..
Watching as my painting drips,
Ink from my pens spill all over,
Papers scattered...
Snakes are quick to hide, these snakes..
Their prey is better off taken at night for,
He is venomous,
She is venomous..
I myself am venomous, hissing for more

Lady of XVIII

As midnight drew
A Lady-in-Waiting sat by her dressing table.
Just fresh eighteen and ready to be another being.
Everyone believes she's angry and cruel
Too hissy and pissy for you,
While she's really numb and deadpanned.

Everyone else is wonderful and grand,
And everyday The Lady-in-Waiting becomes more and more ugly
Since she can't express herself in a way others want.

She wished to cry,
But The Lady didn't know how to.
Uncomfortable by formalities,
Uncomfortable with people she trusts,
Even uncomfortable with the faces of her family.

This Lady, she waits and waits to drown.
Bitterness did not control her,
Nor did her anger, the labels she was called,
The very ones they made her wear..

She wasn't at all what they claimed her to be...
But who would believe the insane Lady who waits,
Then the members of our sane society?

Looping Around the Subway

7:30 am I wake up and try to roll out of bed
I don't really want to go outside today,
The world is full of uncertainty..
But also because I don't really understand myself.
After a bus ride I walk in sync with different people..
I get onto the express train line, I become lost within my empty thoughts..

The train moves fast,
As I wait to approach my stop,
I see different people throughout my ride.
Some reflections of the same,
But we know there is no such thing..
Soon I'm lost at the platforms where my heart was stomped on...

Where do I go from here, school or work?
Or did I just ride the train since I had nothing else to do?
Society has rules that unfairly put us into boxes.
Adults look down on children,
Meanwhile they were once our age
So they should understand the lost feelings we all have at our times of doubt...

People at time shatter and break,
Like a chandelier made of glass..
Breaking allows us to fade away as we go through the day.
We're all simple characters in a storybook,
And life itself unfolds in ongoing chapters..
And I'm still lost on the same platforms with no directions for the future...

Youth is said to be a "gift" because we're young,
But how much longer until I become a true adult?

I wish I could push off this feeling of loneliness,
But how much longer... *Until I can wear that red lipstick?*

Back onto the subways I go,
And sometimes I get lost because all the stops look the same..
It's like getting lost within a crowd where you're unable to make a connection.
The trains don't have souls or voices,
As I'm stuck not wanting to age..
Why was I born into such a fast moving, repeating looping world?

Womanhood - November 20th

A lady who worked for three days,

Clearing off tables for her job

After many hours,

Mind you, it's only her third day of training.

She carried a tray of cups

But they fell and shattered

Blessed that no one got hurt..

But she cried, silently until her shift was over

She did feel bad and was glad no one got hurt,

But she cried, not because she was in trouble,

Or because someone did something wrong in such a positive atmosphere..

She cried mainly because the lady was young,

And it was that time of the month.

She was told it was no big deal,

And tomorrow will be a new day.

But she still cried.

When she left, down the street and on the train until she got home

And her underwear was newly stained red

Trial and Error

So as time went on, I started to look at her in vain.
Blinded not by hate as I still love,
But I couldn't see her in the same light of closeness
After what she said and done.
We were never family because of how
The fires from false fame seemed to consume us.

I roam the earth in lacey white undergarments,
Underneath and black dress and boots
As I roam, I wait for this clinging in my head to fade away..
A bee to be free from anxiety,
Needs to not bother others,
Why can't I flow calmly and carefree like a river?

I have to escape before I while in pure rage
Shall lose all of my modesty..
Forever alone because of fear,
A wicker chair I sit in and mope,
Like an elderly man with no family.
After all this, you still think I'm illiterate.

A Lane of Nothingness

Welcome to nobody's lane
Where each address is a zero.
No self esteem to be found.
As you're buried alive in that dirt that covers the ground
Waiting for something hell-like to just grab you.

What am I during the daylight?
Who I am is just another thing I practiced in the mirror.
Dressed maturely and given jokes,
But in reality, I am sickly and not happy with this attention.
I just want to wear nothing as it's all troublesome.

I never truly lied to you once,
But I will tell you that we all pretend to be different
The moment we first meet as we are unsure if others shall understand.
Beyond your peers, you're just a plot in a cracked photograph,
And I myself will always be a nobody who comes from nothing.

Inside My Heart

We both reached for the object of our desires,
That was of our own decision,
And I'm not sorry
As I sit within my jail cell
Made by my own isolation and unkindness,
Standing tall but still short -

You were selfish for loving me.
I always thought I didn't deserve such.
You gave me a second chance with new hope.
Not faking my feelings and I'm removing my mask.
I will live and I will fight!
I smile as my red heart bleeds from your gunshot -

Was it fate on how we clicked so instantly?
We were nothing but platonic friends.
When I talked to you for some reason...
I was genuine and my true self,
Shedding the layers of my pain.
But why do tears still fall down my face? -

"What were we even thinking?"

You taught me so much and I'm very thankful,
But I only wish that I did the same,
If I changed you one way or another...
I hope it was in a positive light.
You taught me to love myself...
As we both stand together but not on equal platforms -

**"My tears may no longer be red,
But my heart that once bled is.."**

74 - Harley Rose

Day IV

The love interest is Sir Nicholas himself.
He is tall and fit,
His eyes are of a pained soul,
Death's sorrow tells us he is kind and loving,
It's his job no one likes except for I,
Upon my coffin is where I lay,
Tonight's the night.
He comes to me,
Whispers in my ear,
He isn't a bad one,
It's just hard to say "goodbye",
To someone you thought you loved.

Euphoria Is

I'm having an affair with my past,
And my future must never know.
It was bitter the sound of cheerfulness
And the feeling of relief was sour.
The elf plays his flute
And the fairy strums her lute,
Luring us into faking emotions.
The youth in the light is so tragic.
Very rebellious that it paints the walls red,
As a sound bounces, two souls connect
Without a wire, I can't wait to meet them...
As I look and apply my lipstick, my mirror is cracked
I don't really mind if the made up illusion is distorted
And your eyes fell in love with the truth of my words..
Smiles are nothing but tears unsalted
Since your wound is still fresh

Self Satisfaction

Growing up to the point
Where my dress is too short..
Then again today everything is modest.
All creatures have eyes that need to allure grace,
Different pleasures for all, everybody has what they like
Even what they dislike,
Scandalous is could be
Fined by twilight, smells of what they're passionate about.

Panting heavily by the windows light
Bees buzz towards the flowers,
But what if the bees couldn't find a flower?
Would they go find a bluejay or a robin?
They hum as they begin to think
Heavy but quieter their thoughts become..
The pleasure of one's own is new

Who needs a flower?
Why did a bee need a bird?
What flower needs a bee?
What a confusing and bumpy ride..
Bees and Flowers continue to be together,
When they find that they cannot be,
When the animal is in the mood
Sometimes, self satisfaction can be most worthy...

Señor Esperanza y Señorita Sueño

Para un hombre, su nombre era Esperanza.

Para una mujer, su nombre era Sueño.

Se conocieron una noche por la fe,

Esperanza, se sentó en la arena

Vistiendo todo de negro

Su capa de botas junto a él y su sombrero estaba en su mano.

Observando el océano bajo un cielo estrellado.

Más feliz en su faz y Sueño,

llevaba un vestido de seda rosa,

Sosteniendo sus zapatos

Ella caminó por la orilla

Su la tela del rosa aparece en sus ojos,

Le ofreció un asiento.

A ninguno de los dos les gustaron sus nombres,

Pero dijeron con confianza

Sus nombres el uno al otro.

Juntos tomados de la mano se pusieron de pie

Y caminamos juntos hacia el mar

Señor Esperanza y Señorita Sueño

Desaparecieron juntos

Mano a mano.. Para vigilar la corriente

'No se habla de esa como *"¿Qué amas?"'*

Pero velar por las personas que tienen esperanzas y sueños

The Evil One

The Evil One snarls
He has me within his grip,
He makes me feel uncomfortable
Yet I am still intrigued, but why?

I won't allow him to have my mind,
I shall fight such elements of dark power he spreads
Sadly, the demons always come back.

The isolation I have made for myself,
Despite its pain I rather express and feel that,
Then have my heart ripped out by you
At least the Evil One understands me.

I'm branded as an "outcast" by those who don't get me,
Why waste my energy on anyone at all then?
Even my own mother drains me almost as bad as the Evil One.

When order becomes chaos,
I shall find peace with myself and my demons.
The room I'm in is pitch black, I'm scared..
Confidently I won't let Him know that!

Screaming outrageously but not in anger or pain,
I don't care if He punishes me for disobeying,
If he wishes to rule me then he better overthrow me!

Seven Perfection

Walking through a dimmed hallway,
Rose petals fall to my feet
Seven perfect petals within my long locks
Some red, some pink, some yellow..
As I turn the corner,
I enter a room with all my friends
I ignore them, for I am lost in thought
Some are gambling playing cards,
Using a "sixth sense"
The count down to be perfectly imperfect
Began once we were born..
Dreams change. Dreams stay the same..
Someone called out my name,
I turned and faced them
"one or eight" he said
"Why not seven perfection?" I asked..
"Because seven is a perfectly imperfect number
Eight is perfect and even" he responded.
I turned around and kept walking..
He stood there confused,
I walked back into the dimmed hallway,
Which is stained with roses upon the walkway

Cos and Sin

A world connected by a traced line will become your musical audience..
Much similar to how the Earth and Sun connect with one another
Light and Shadow will now be contrasting as we begin using metaphors...
While staring in this Black and White silent film
You can only see the shade of my bloody red lipstick.

Science dominates us with theories and facts that we believe to be true,
But who for sure can say that they are?
The tree of life, the biology of humanity,
Reflects the whispers from the workplace gossip.
Emotions can't be defined by a simple hypothesis or diagnosis.

As we fall in love along your leather chair within the shadows,
Seductively you'll soon place a gold chain around my neck..
Just as the clock begins once more,
We're crumbling to grasp what's fantasy and what's reality,
Nothing will be forever which can bring fights between one another.

Remember back in class when we learned
'How gratify defines the laws of physics,
With the rotations and revolutions of life'?
Now they cannot come between us even as the floor disappears
Allowing us to fall deeper into the unknown, you're a terrible influencer

Chaotic Means

With just one chaotic war victory,
One that brings a worldwide new year of pride..
Bathing in the blood of past veins,
Soap made from my last olive branch,
Brings new faith after the dirty ones were washed away.

'Who are you?' I asked the likeness in the river,
For it's not my own, it belongs to another.
I fear beyond the shallowness of my pity woes.
So why not come and take my breath away,
And we'll spring into the mountains of unpredictability.

Sorrow still follows me like a shadow,
An answer is what I am waiting for..
But a room full of grandma's old lullabies is what I get.
Yet what is it I wish to gain a future from?
A birth of love or a path of bliss in anger.

Hold me as I go blind,
For I will no longer see what will pain me..
Our fingers are interwoven as my screams reach the clouds for heaven.
I wish for a happy call,
With a chaotic victory at its core.

First Love

One love, a first love.
A heart for a flirtatious crush
It's wild at first,
Like a jungle infested,
Or a Café that's booming but is short staffed.
My heart stops,
I see him.. does he see me?
Should I wish to stay friends
Before I decide on a final goodbye?
Oy, if I knew I'd feel this way,
I wouldn't have shared that dance with him.

Our Privilege Minority

Sometimes I get such bad anxiety,
That my chest hurts,
It feels as if a knife is stabbing me
And I am ready to drop dead on the street.

Panic attacks beyond compared
"You just turned 18 live a little" they say,
But how can I live on with so much noise in my way?

Humans are too much,
Even when they state they care for others
They'll still put you in harm's way.

Freedom isn't a choice.
It's a privilege, a right that was given,
Yet stolen to many in our racist history.
Today, all humans have a right.

But the spirals of life always seem to get in the way.
Both my middle fingers raised to the sky,
Black boots laced up..

I stand in the middle of the road
Holding up traffic,
"You, human, should have killed me when you had the chance"
I say to them all...

Anne

Black out shadows and a smoky stage,
Despite the girl wearing a pink floral peasant dress,
Fishnet stockings and black boots were worn with...
Her hair was dyed purple.
Eyeliner was painted thick.

My garden of solitude
Guarded heavily by many soldiers
Hundreds of rows and rows of different flowers,
Live lovely along with the sound of a mandolin!
Once the violins start to play, everything begins to rot.

As all individuals are beautiful and rare..
Her music screams out lyrics,
The very ones that brings terror towards all normies.
And bright colors are desired to be matched with black..
Nature is soft, a beauty taken for granted.

Skulls with ripped jeans and nails painted,
Dragon leggings with plaid skirts and funky hair,
Flowers with boots roaming the woods,
With the smoke from fire in the backyard alley,
I'm where I belong, with Anne

Ghosting

Can you hear me?
I reach out to tap your arm,
But my hand goes straight through.
How odd yet to the point.

Can you see me?
There is no goal to be found,
There is no love to hold onto.
I wouldn't want to save my own skin.

Will you stay with me?
Even as the candles burn low,
Each petal on my roses begin to wilt.
Fate plays a role in our game of life.

Why do I feel empty?
Too light to dent the earth,
Weighing next to none...
When you're put to lay you'll feel empty too.

Society's Party

A girl lost out in the snow,
Within the forest,
She finds a tiny house,
But it's not what it appears to be,
She gently begins knocking on the door -

"What is it that you want?" thought the annoyed owner,
Soon the girl entered and spoke...
"Hello, is anyone here?"
"Do you need something? Help?"
She turned in shocked
She saw me, a puppet with strings.. a mobile doll
Everyone and everything dressed as if it's 1907! But modern too..
"Do you see something you like?"
As a creepy song begins to play off the music box,
My wooden body begins to walk towards her..
The Society Party has started!
With everyone in the house pulling the girl to warmth,
Trying to change her attire and pouring tea,
Some with wine in their glasses,
For playtime won't begin until we start a fire...
With everyone dressed so differently,
But often in dark colors to match their ghostly auras.
This world is full of lies...
This home is a dollhouse with Marionettes..
They sing, dance, skip and have very merry days!
It's like the happiness of desires,
But it's also nothing but an experience of torture -

Batting my lashes,
Smiling, I am bad with a big heart..

The girl fell asleep,

But morning never came

"Shall I tell you a secret as your hostess?

Take a look at the clock girly, it has no hands…"

She screamed, for boxes for each of us puppets,

Looking like coffins

"Mornings never come to the dollhouse..

Only do full moon evenings"

As we sit at the tea table,

We have tea and play dolls

Like how life and society attaches us to strings..

We're all puppets playing a role..

The girl seemed very frightened

"Don't be scared…"

She looked confused as our male host popped in,

"Even if we are free to have a personality and voices

We're not at all free.

So we're all puppets chained to 'life'.

Puppets to ourselves and each other.

It's not that we want to be but we are

It's just one of the unwritten rules,

Especially when ignorance and guilt continues to live on!" -

Please, keep away because I am a monster..

I, Harley, am a wooden doll.

Wearing gothic appeal yet bright floral dresses,

Attached to strings and wearing dark makeup..

Boots and my hair topped with a bow..

You can never love me..

As I bend you look at me lovingly..

I'm not innocent,

I'm no fun,
I'm not at all completely sane,
I'm just a rebellious marionette!
Nothing special is to happen..
It's already dawn.
The doors of the dollhouse are beginning to close.
"You better leave before you're locked in," someone called.
As the clock without hands chims,
The bells ring, ding, ling and ring, shaking the whole house.
And the girl tries to run as fast as her legs would carry..
The male host takes off his top hat,
He holds his pocket watch with his other hand
As the whole world unconsciously spins.

Sadly, the girl never did make it out in time...
She became a puppet to our Society's Party
The lights dimmed,
The house is once again quiet..
Play Time's Over for now..

My Muse

How far can I go until I find the voice I searched for
Where has my muse for art gone?
A nosy city I live within,
I rather die than live someplace else

A man I saw from a far yet I knew my words
Could not be inspired by him
A male, untrue because my eyes lie to me.
I can't bear to be seen before noon.

Which must be why I feel righteously
When I hide behind my pen.
I hide behind my glorious paint brush,
Obnoxiously I skip in fashion I am without..

Funny one minute, obviously the next.
My home isn't a place for dreams, no muses come to me.
For we don't have the time for such fairytales...
A muse with no inspiration I seem to be.

Always have your Wit while in Battle

I hold my sword as if I'm ready to strike!
Your eyes are nothing but teasing me,
And all alone I thought I would be
In a place where nothing but drunken noise roams.
It remains a mystery on why
Medieval fashion covers our skins alike.
Where once the forest burns,
The famous flames that caused you to lose me,
It won't happen tonight.
Lustful I wish I could be,
You see beneath the mask I practiced for hours,
When I dolled myself up.
I'll soon run as quick as the wind,
To the smell of rum and where the sounds of our swords clashing
We fight as if we're dancing in this sketchy tavern.
What a row it caused,
It's all thanks to my witty personality.

Am I Your Imperial View

If I was perfect,
If I was your ideal,
Would I still ramble on in a conversation?

And would I always be kept locked behind a wall?
Would I be able to truly like myself,
If I was true perfection?
Oh, how terrible I feel for the most gentle women in history.

No flaws to crack,
And society's faults wouldn't harm me
Even if I wear the same uniform as everyone else..

I blend in with the crowd,
Except for my hair being cut raggedy,
Once I dyed my hair purple
Always had eyeliner tracing my eyes..

If I was smart would I know if I could trust you or not?
If I was Miss Perfect would I truly fade into the crowd,
Like how I do now while I'm imperfect?

My Reclusive Heart

My heartbeats when you walk up to me
And I forget what words were flowing in my mind
Don't let my talkative side misled you,
I'm a rather reclusive person.
I will not speak about my childhood,
To stay hidden I wear all black
Fading into the crowd I so badly despise,
The one I was once murdered in...
As a fight begins so easily,
As my voice roams volumes max
My heartbeat breaks since I wished for love,
Something in anger I'll never truly possess

Mirror oh Mirror

When I look in the mirror,
I don't see someone I like — in appearance or personality.
I don't see someone I think I know.
I'm afraid of the silver chain that hangs around my neck

I would no longer be intimidated by you
Whether you're my boss or not.
My reflection will be of someone I like,
And the mirror then will become my friend..

I Thank the Almighty

The sunlight peeked through my closed curtains,
My bedroom is cluttered yet I must put on my uniform.
Comfortable yes, conformity no thanks.
I walk — all within a rainy day, what a hazy sun shower.
As I smelled the fresh flowers,
The sky shouted at me "Time to go, it's magically"
Where? To a place beyond just realism,
Only for fantasy to play a piano tune,
It barks such a tune the flute could whirl.
Bells ring and I become composed with myself.
A single paint brush ; A single canvas
I only own a drop of paint.
So I use it sparingly — as if it was my last sip of water,
If I were to walk the desert
For miles and the long years
With nowhere to roam, like Merlin.
I thank the almighty for a color to keep me collected,
This drop of paint is my holy grail!
I must create everything and make a speech to share.
I can make something real, but I prefer not to.
We'll dance to the night and paint the sun anew
As many people beautifully shine through

Sunlight

Look into the sun
Where the sunflowers grow.
I struggle as the vines wrap themselves around me,
Holding me back,
They're too tight to break.
The race has already begun,
Despite no 'Ready, Set, Go!' being called.
Blinded by pollen.
Consumed by tiredness..
I don't wish to be an innocent lily,
I want to be a weed,
So that I'll grow back stronger
Especially when you cut me down.
Life isn't a garden,
It's a war that never ends.

Adulting is False

Beyond the hills you'll walk,

Each folk in the road,

With many tribulations

The stars will breathe for you and I..

At night, I can't help but have my heart ache

I go to my old hang out — the full moon shines

Owls hoot and everyone who loves the dark side gathers together.

As the skeletons whistle at me

And the wind that howls.

The many graves have spirits sitting upon them,

Gossiping and laughing as if they still live on.

Wanting me to stay in the shadows

Loving them forever

Like that 'faze' I had in High School,

I honestly never grew out of

But to succeed in life

A floral falsehood I must live

Existence

Life works with an unfamiliar bliss
What you and I think we know
With nothing but tears becoming laughs.
Yesterday will not be remembered,
Tomorrow is unknown
Today will be forgotten.
And we will live with a memorized folder.

Life isn't as open minded as you and I
I have no memories to press together,
It's all cluttered and in a blur.
Why must we come and go?
Lies told as a child,
Truths told as an adult.
It's no good when I tell you I wish to be perfection.

Life works without true justice
What you and I think we own
Only leaves nothing but scars,
In our pockets and hearts
As if we're nothing at all.
Not even Miriam could've had a heart of gold.
Let's just sit on the park swings and look solemn.

The Optical Fool

I woe, due to this truthful optical illusion,
It tells me the lie that is us
Performers in a mockery of the theater we named "Living"
And where no kaleidoscope can save me,
I'll forever be a mystery for the world,
A grand question you'll never be able to mark or grade.

What do you wish to understand about me?
I'm humorously hungry,
But there are so many paths in front of me...
Yet people stand in my way.
And the broken system is missing out due to flaws it cannot accept.
You'll look back at me and a storm of rage builds up inside.

I know that I am a disappointment to you..
So I walk the nights alone like always,
A fresh breeze blows in my face, it's so satisfying.
To know who I am is all I ask for..
Yet society will forever be a party of unkindness.
Your eyes have gone blind the minute you look at me.

You can't tell me what to do as I'm a rebellious child...
And I'll laugh, as your words escape my ears
I never caught what you said,
Which is alright, since your words were universally accepted by all but me.
A fool you became by following me around all lovesick like —
I promise you that I'll achieve greatness even if it's small to the eye of the fool.

Yellow Flowers, oh how I envy them

Sunflowers, I envy them
Since they're always staring at the sun
The very one that's high in the sky.
Where daylight breaks
In the field where we stay,
A little weed I am - Stubborn and Proud.
Despite this, I'm wounded like a bird with a broken wing.

To me, sunflowers don't need a therapy session,
But who am I to say so otherwise..
Unprepared for the world we both are,
In spite of this tragic predicament
Only one of us wears a bright colored coat
In this damaging world
To survive I must paint my face for all to see.

In ten years from now I fear –
That I too will be a sunflower.
And people like to say I'm a butterfly,
Or a petal, blossoming to full bloom.
No one knows the ever changing formations I go through,
And at night I can't help but think
'What did I do to make her so mad?'

Orchestra

Her voice was that of an angel,
It was so beautiful to my ears.
Yes, she couldn't hold a note when she sang.
It was alluring that I wanted her to talk to me forever and ever.

Together, me and her are like an orchestra,
Sparks fly as the sounds of hundreds of instruments soar,
And I realized she is who I wanted,
Yet she didn't want me in that way, a rainbow road I walk.

And as all the once cheerful and lively music
Became nothing but pain filled and mournful,
The violins now cry, and each instrument follows
The Orchestra became nothing but a depressing pit

Innocence

A little lily floats above the water.
What a sense of tranquility,
One that people often take for granted.
With their bitter taste on beauty
Nature is a kind of being
Without it how can we grow and learn?
We might be in the big city,
Where buildings grow and grow -
Fast moving pace makes people walk..
But for one second, just a second
Let's walk the ground spiritual
All of us can be our own lily,
Our own flower that can float away.
Peacefully and detached from worry

Are There Two? — Two That Are True?

The boats sailed

For all to see — find a new

To travel for three but to ask

"Are there two?

Two that are true?"

Sailors sang and swayed on deck

For logical brains and wine to drink

At a party unlike the others.

My gown floats around as if it's dances,

As I climb the stairs from waves to the clouds.

Slim hips, survived the war

The many fevers of childbirths wail,

Miracles and careful breachers

For all but two,

When one omen is true,

Another follows like a weed in the graveyard.

Hyacinth

Falling into many hysterics,
Where many wisteria's bloom.
The wedding bells toll,
Dressed in a gown of glory,
But to achieve such a familiar memory
For once all confidence in one's view
Yet the warmth is fading
As one's feather wings turn to yellow ember flames.

I've grown too old for much,
And at times I do feel as if I'm trapped.
One could say that I'm locked in a cage deep under the sea.
A storm waves and blows,
That storm — wasting its heavy breaths,
I walk slowly as everyone else is soaring.

On a winter night —
A night where flare is dramatically angered.
A nightmare this wedding day has become.
Wednesday isn't one of true sorrow,
So let's get married on that day.
This Wednesday, and the next Wednesday,
Let's propose a new way to achieve graceful lust.
Trust me as we fall to the dark side

I'm lost in a garden covered in fog,
Where tulips sing, petunias dance, violets mourn and poppy's play,
But my name is given in romantic vain
Florals all in dressed royally to imposed
So that talent is what I wish to have
My wedding bells allow a nightmare to become one with heaven.

Angels Venom

Lord Death came knocking on my door,
Like he does every month.
He refuses to take me home with him — to the castle.
He just wants a drink with me as he increases his debts.

He always brings me white lilies,
Mankind being so misleading..
One doesn't care if another is either happy or not
So why should I be nice to him?

With his wispy and boneless fingers
The King tries to choke me
But with no waves to roar
He can't take me even if I beg.

No dark thoughts I am allowed to have.
It's not safe to share or reach for help.
No hope to swim with the sirens that call,
And no bath is truly calming.

He wouldn't accept me,
Angels watching over me while I want a demon to follow me
Since I'll never be happy in this world
I am forced to work and educate myself to survive reality.

My Letter to the World

My letter to the world will never be understood by all..
As I sense a change in the wind
One where all inner scars become —
Inside out, showing themselves to the world.
Where I once lost my sanity,
Still in this maze of the terror
I brought on, love was lost to all.
Order was forgotten,
Words were said in all honesty.
Blood was sadly shed in secret.
I gave up on everyone, including myself.
I am young and lively,
But who truly is selfish, you or I?
I think at this darling hour,
We're not meant for tomorrow
To just wait for hell and everything
To separate us..
Especially since we don't know one thing about one another
Yet we've been living together since forever,
It was made of dysfunction but was also a home to me

Half Empty

There is this emptiness that plagues me
As I lose all interest in what I love,
And I forget all the aspects I once learned.
One night, I tried to remember all the good times that passed,
But it all came back numb.
"You're young. Enjoy your youth"
"I was once depressed too"
"It's all in your head."
"There isn't a reason for you to be sad"
"That's your baggage"
These things people say,
It only makes me feel worse.
I'm forever in a funk
Even on my good days I think...
If I act happy, social, and fun
I can hide the fact that I want to run and hide.
This irritable and tired feeling overcomes me
I can't help but get annoyed at every little thing,
Except for the sounds that come from nature,
I wonder 'when did I lose all hope?'

Breathing in Claustrophobia

A bird stalked me when I walked the city
To be a question without an answer
I'll never be what you wished
Even when you look to the Delta Aquarius for hope.

So, please just allow me to get lost in the world that harms me
Who am I? Please help me understand who I am..
But if you'd help me, I would then hate you more.
It's just how I roll.

People often make me feel claustrophobic.
The world spins on an axel,
The sun gives the beautiful moon light
And people who speak are nothing but forgetful, almost unimportant like me.

Stories I tell, all honest and strange
I never had a place I like to call home,
Even my childhood home makes me feel out of place
I sometimes can't even look my Ursa Major in the face.

An empty road I walk at night,
To the world I'm invisible, especially in the rain
And we're soaked and lost by what's present in our respective lives
As we try to escape this in closed space that antagonizes me

Holding Up the Train

Life isn't fun without a person who's unconventional.
Let's remove that veil since it hides too much.
The view made by the painter,
His model will be the world's future landscape.
Together we watched as the sky opened up
I wandered off to think about that one blue dress in the shop window..
What made it so beautiful?

Now I walk day after day down the same old street,
Onto the train tracks — I am holding up the ride to oddly enjoy this view.
What is the meaning of pure euphemism?
Everyone is beautiful..
And Discord will become your one true friend.
That one song that led me to fall smitten wasn't even grand.
What is it that makes me a joke to society?
My top hat or my hair? My fashion?
Was it my accent or my personality?
What was it?

People always seem either annoyed or indifferent with me,
I'm the life of the party and of the funeral.
Down right depressing it is
Morphing into something new won't change these facts.
Plaid skirts, pants too big, and floral blouses..
Sometimes I just want to shave my head,
Sing to mental and bang my head! -

As I walk day after day down the same old street
Onto the train tracks — I am holding up the ride to cry out my sorrow
I want to end it all and even more..
I am in men's trousers being held up by suspenders.

As I wonder what it would be like to be normal,
Your voice led me to fall into a smitten trap.
The others around me are dressed in lace and pretty dresses.
At night I would climb to my roof
So I could hope, dream and cry alone,
So that I wouldn't appear weak in your eyes!

The Month of Terrors

Snapping my fingers as many boogie
To the sound of wild birds and heavy laughter in the lunar night
Surprised beyond another ingredient on this night.
The wind told my ears of a story would make me shake in fear
Yet, all I got was a woe and a realization that I am tired..

A pool of my own tears and fears drown as I hold my teddy bear close.
Clowns laughing beyond their circus trail
Skeletons shimmering in the playground
Zombies crawling towards you for a snack
Blood trails the back of her nightdress.

Where wedding bells ring
The roaring hours are long over.
Years that came have gone by
And I've gotten afraid of the same everyday things.
My heart is so old that it doesn't matter..

I'll scare you if I must!
I long for something special though..
Witches on brooms looking for gossip from the garden.
Boats crash as the bank goes bankrupt
Losing all in the fog of screams.

Doctors murdering creepily,
He once was such a handsome patient.
Roaming the damage of the lake posters.
Ghosts haunt me in a good way, they give me luck..
But my dreams tragically hover over me with their voiceless corruption.

I grew bored of the darkness.
It kept me away from those unknown
While it's the warmth I love most of all,
The darkness that roamed made me feel like I belong
But it pulls me away from sinful light.

Togetherness is a Whole

Let's be euphoric together,
What a fake security it could be.
He knocks on my floor,
My hallucinations roam free after years of being trapped..
As we sleep together in our dark aesthetic

Let's be platonic together,
What benefits it could bear.
My father abandoned all but I
Since I've never known the awful man.
This is where we both understand the word 'broken'

Let's get lost in life together,
With an abstract insecurity we could create.
Mental death is painful and it leaves us out of place,
Could real freedom come sooner than we expect?
This pain is also numb as its all a blur

Fairytale Creatures

The sunlight peeked through my closed curtains,
All within a rainy day,
What a hazy sun shower.
Such a tune the riddler of a fiddle could play.
Wouldn't you agree when it's combined with a flute?

I decided to take a stroll
Paint stained my skin
My clothing was losing its pigment.
As the rain washed it away —
The world is being painted

If I were to walk the desert
For miles treasuring years,
With nowhere to roam, like Merlin.
My mistakes, misery and all the things
Haunt me as pixies play

A heavenly kiss of growth that came on the eclipse
Where the leap year grows in the funhouse of mirrors
Silver siblings dance a ballet,
Sirens wail for diamond waves
And elves live in my room of nature..

The sun shines brightly
As rain comes down hard,
We'll dance together — not jump, dance together
As we swirl as color magically grows and expands
For an eclipse like no other will appear tonight.

Vexing

You're so vex, then again I am so sorry
Soulless you are
I refuse to use you.
Pathetic I may be — but alone you'll always be.
I'm content with myself.
You can't be true.
I'm lazy? I live in filth?
Yes I do, the filth from one's mouth to my ears
Is what I live in.
With dysfunctional unfairness
Who uses fear and control,
Herself, is selfish and lazy.
I can be rude too,
Then again I don't wish to be like you.
So I bid you farewell, my dearest.
I rather kill myself than hear from you.
Since you're the true slob,
Not in home or hospitality but in mind and growth.

My Eye and You

I stab a pen in my eye
So that I couldn't see
Forget what should be
We were just plain lost
In the garden of false lovers
My Eye sees You,
But do you see my eye?

As our illness grew graver
We found ourselves with lips that locked
In fear we grant
We're losing ourselves in what should have always been
A day in wondrous misery

Eema's Raizels Gave Me My Name

These words I spoke
Were all my own.
In real life I'm unpredictable, natural and honest.
You'd never know what I'll say,
But on paper — I'm raw and vulnerable.

A flower I despise, one that brings me disinterest
Despite me loving all parts of nature's grace.
A woman who gave me life
Her favorite flower is that, a rose.
I named myself after her own favorite floral.

To inspire the world with my twisted words..
Her flower gave me my pen,
The world will think we're close —
We are to a point yet creative differences blind us
A dysfunctional love can never truly be unbroken.